Base-Ball Ballads

The McFarland Historical Baseball Library

1. Cobb, Ty. *Busting 'Em and Other Big League Stories* (1914). 2003
2. Axelson, G.W. *"Commy": The Life Story of Charles A. Comiskey* (1919). 2003
3. Ellard, Harry. *Base Ball in Cincinnati: A History* (1907). 2004
4. Richter, Francis C. *Richter's History and Records of Base Ball, the American Nation's Chief Sport* (1914). 2005
5. Lanigan, Ernest J. *Baseball Cyclopedia* (1922). 2005
6. Evers, John J., and Hugh S. Fullerton. *Touching Second* (1910). 2005
7. Rice, Grantland. *Base-Ball Ballads* (1910). 2005
8. Claudy, C.H. *The Battle of Base-Ball* (1912). 2005
9. Kelly, Mike "King." *"Play Ball": Stories from the Diamond Field and Other Historical Writings about the 19th Century Hall of Famer* (1888). 2006.
10. Anonymous and Noah Brooks. *The Great Match* [1877] *and Our Base Ball Club* [1884]*: Two Novels from the Early Days of Base Ball*, volume editors Trey Strecker and Geri Strecker. 2010
11. Green, Guy W. *The Nebraska Indians* [1900] *and Fun and Frolic with an Indian Ball Team* [1907]*: Two Accounts of Baseball Barnstorming at the Turn of the Twentieth Century*, volume editor Jeffrey P. Beck. 2010
12. Salsinger, H.G. *Ty Cobb: Two Biographies—"Our Ty: Ty Cobb's Life Story" (1924) and "Which Was Greatest: Ty Cobb or Babe Ruth?" (1951)*, volume editor William R. Cobb. 2012
13. Joss, Addie. *Addie Joss on Baseball: Collected Newspaper Columns and World Series Reports, 1907–1909*, compiled and annotated by Rich Blevins. 2012

Base-Ball Ballads

by Grantland Rice

Illustrated by C.H. Wellington

McFarland Historical Baseball Library, 7
Gary Mitchem *and* Mark Durr, *Editors*

McFarland & Company, Inc., Publishers
Jefferson, North Carolina, and London

ISBN 0-7864-2038-3 (softcover : 50# alkaline paper) ∞

Library of Congress cataloguing data are available

British Library cataloguing data are available

On the cover: Grantland Rice
(National Baseball Hall of Fame Library, Cooperstown, N.Y.)

Manufactured in the United States of America

McFarland & Company, Inc., Publishers
Box 611, Jefferson, North Carolina 28640
www.mcfarlandpub.com

DEDICATED TO THE FAN

From lowly bootblack of the town
To merchant prince of high renown,
Or butcher, baker, candle-maker,
Lawyer, doctor, undertaker,
Priest or farmer, young or old,
Or rich or poor within the fold,
So that his spirit bows before
The Bondage of the full box score—
Whatever be his name or fame,
So that his heart leans to the GAME

Contents

Contents

Editors' Note

Today a target for critics of the "Gee Whiz" school of sportswriting and popular or sentimental verse, Grantland Rice was immensely popular in his day, both with the public and other writers. He was by all accounts a learned man, one who credited his facile versifying to an affinity for scanning the classical poets and who made Latin oratorical structure a hallmark of his columns. Yet he was decidedly unpretentious, identifying "the great mass of the public" for his audience and refusing to ascribe literary value to anything he wrote. And what he wrote was made available almost daily to his readers, first in the regional papers of the South and Midwest, then the Northeast, and finally, beginning in 1914, across the country in syndication.

Henry Grantland Rice was born in Murfreesboro, Tennessee, in 1880. He graduated from Vanderbilt University, where he captained both the baseball and football teams and received degrees in Greek and Latin. After commencement, he turned down a professional baseball contract from the Southern Association's Nashville Vols and began his journalism career with the *Nashville Daily News,* covering the courts and local politics as well as sports. Almost immediately he began to liven his commentary with verse, an approach peculiar to the era and shared by a number of other well-known journalists of the day, including Franklin P. Adams, Eugene Field, Judd Mortimer Lewis and Don Marquis. His success with the so-called verse-and-paragraph style led to recognition and stints at the *Atlanta Journal* and the *Cleveland News*, after which he returned to Nashville, taking up the position of sports editor for the *Tennessean* in 1907.

It was during his tenure at the *Tennessean* that Rice stepped up his production of verse, which was published not on the sports pages, generally, but in a daily column for the editorial page titled "Tennessee 'Uns." (His responsibilities at the paper were numerous and required long hours.) According to biographer Charles Fountain, Rice produced nearly a quarter of his poetry in the four years he was with the *Tennessean,* generating "a minimum of 24 lines of verse a day."

By 1910, Rice had both a backlog of poems and regional readership sufficient for the *Tennessean* to publish *Base-Ball Ballads,* which included 57 rhymed poems written in a wide variety of meters and forms. Among the best known are parodies, including three involving Ernest Thayer's Casey: "Casey's Revenge," "Mudville's Fate," and "The Man Who Played with Anson on the Old Mudville Team." (The latter, Fountain points out, not only recycles the Casey character but mimics the style of Eugene Field's "The Man Who Worked with Dana on the Noo York Sun.") Rice also parodied Longfellow's "Paul Revere's Ride" ("The Slide of Paul Revere"), Poe's "The Raven" ("The Raven Up-to-Date"), Kipling's "Mandalay" ("On the Road to Rooters' Row"), and Ben King's "The Ghost" ("The Shock"). Among the real life players and baseball personalities identified by name in this collection of poems are Cy Young, Honus Wagner, Ty Cobb, Cap Anson, Kid Eberfeld, George Van Haltren, Christy Mathewson, Ed Reulbach, Ed Plank, Hughie Jennings, Silk O'Loughlin,

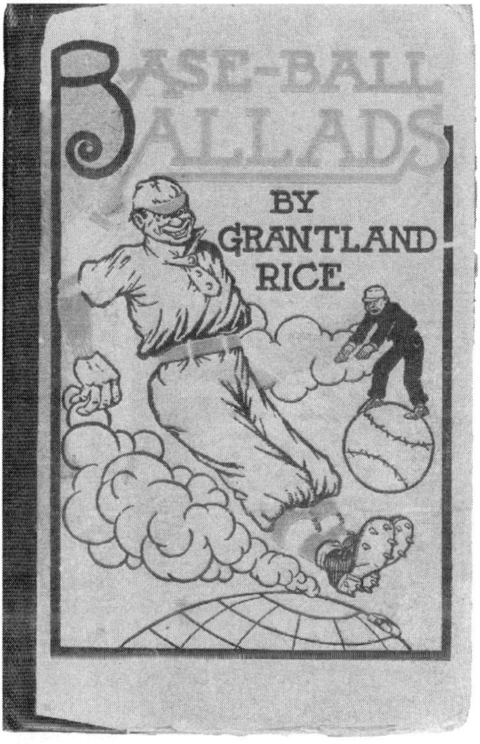

C.H. Wellington's cover illustration for the 1910 edition of *Base-Ball Ballads*.

John Clarkson, Amos Rusie, John McGraw and Noodles Hahn.

The book includes a recognizable refrain about the proper spirit of competition: "Nor victory, nor yet defeat / is chalked against the player's name, / but down the roll the final scroll / shows only 'how he played the game.'" Though these lines from "Game Called" are strongly associated with baseball and Babe Ruth's death, the sentiment was made famous in a couplet from the 1908 occasional poem "Alumnus Football": "For when the One Great Scorer comes to mark against your name / He writes—not that you won or lost—but how you played the Game." His work toward this expression of the idea dates to at least 1907, in the poem "Out on the Lines," included in *Base-Ball Ballads.* Interestingly, two additional poems in the volume wrestle with precisely the same idea and in nearly the same words, "Play Ball" and "The Test." It was only in 1948 that the poem "Game Called" was revised for the occasion of Babe Ruth's death.

In 1913, Rice wrote the first of his syndicated Sportlight columns;

he wrote his last more than forty years later on July 13, 1954, the day of his death. In between he voiced the first radio broadcast of a World Series game, in 1922; co-created the Sportlight Films production company and was nominated for six Academy Awards, winning two as a producer; and published 14 other books, including four more collections of poetry. *Base-Ball Ballads* remained his only book exclusively about baseball.

The book's illustrator, Charles H. Wellington—nicknamed "Duke"—was born in St. Louis, Missouri, in 1884. He started his cartooning career in 1908, working for the *Memphis News-Scimitar*. While there he caught the attention of newspaper tycoon Henry Stoddard, who offered him a job at the *New York Evening Mail*. He would later move to Los Angeles and while there worked as a gag writer for the Hal Roach Studios. Wellington's contribution to comic art included a single panel cartoon called "—and the Worst Is Yet to Come," which ran from 1913 to 1916, but it was his comic strip "Pa's Son-in-Law," created in 1914, that was his lasting legacy. The strip ran until Wellington's death in 1942.

Published before Rice had achieved a national reputation as a versifier, *Base-Ball Ballads* soon fell out of print and has become increasingly rare. The McFarland edition exactly reproduces the text of the original, including any peculiarities of spelling and punctuation. The pagination has been adjusted to fit series specifications; in some instances the change has affected the line turns of the poems, restoring for some the breaks Rice intended. C.H. Wellington's illustrations have been re-sized, including the title-page illustration for both editions, which depicts an umpire standing atop a baseball. A first-line and title index and this editorial note have been added. Any additional modifications are enclosed in brackets.

The editors gratefully acknowledge the assistance of Joanne Kemp, adult services librarian of the Ashe County (N.C.) Library, and Pam Mitchem, instructor and assistant archivist at Appalachian State University. Both accommodated frequent (and sometimes last-minute) research requests and interlibrary loan orders.

Gary Mitchem
Mark Durr

Base-Ball Ballads.

PLAY BALL.

"PLAY ball"—across the field of green
  The signal sounds the game again;
Once more there reels across the scene
  The shout and wild acclaim again;
The game is on, the fight begun,
  Across the line of battle's span
Until the final score is spun
  With every record of the clan.

"Play ball"—the reveille has rolled
  The bugle call to play again;
Once more beneath the banner's fold
  They troop across the way again;
The game is on, and in the fray
  The tumult and the cheering sweep
Across the battle line of play
  Until the twilight shadows creep.

"Play ball"—the slogan of the game
  Of life, of war, of love or hate;
For rank or wealth, for name or fame
  The player stands against the plate;
The game is on, and in the strife
  Where Fate, the pitcher, speeds the ball
The player plays the game of life
  Until the final shadows fall.

WHEN THE BUG IS ON THE BAWL.

COME, sing ye, Jimmy Riley, from your ancient lyric stock,
"When the frost is on the pumpkin and the fodder's in the shock,"
And we'll let the bounding echoes catch the lyric in your lay
As it darts around the bases to the outfield and away;
For there's music in its make-up and there's rhythm in its run,
With a touch of "back to nature" in its sentiment of fun.
But in some way it has struck us that the theme is out of date,
As a new age comes a-whizzing and a-curving by the plate;
So we'll start another chorus as the echoes rise and fall:
"When the bat is on the bingle and the bug is on the bawl."

Come, sing ye, Jimmy Riley, and we'll listen to your strain,
But we find our thoughts a-straying from the waving of the grain
To the waving of the bludgeons as the batters draw 'em back,
And they wave against the trade-mark with a wallop and a whack,
And "the swimmin' hole" is faded, with its one-time tender pull,

To the "hole" the pitcher's got in with the bloomin'
bases full;
And while, whatever happens, we will never have a
knock
For the "frost upon the pumpkin and the fodder in the
shock,"
There's a later theme that draws us where the echoes
rise and fall.
When the bat is on the bingle and the bug is on the
bawl.

So come ye, Jimmy Riley, with a later song to sing:
"When the fan is on the frolic and the wallop on the
wing,
When the swing is on the spitter and the swipe is on
the swat,
When the bum is on the bobble and he boots one
round the lot,
When the break is on the bender and the squad is on
the slump,
Or the flag is on the flutter and the brick is on the
ump."
Belay that ancient chatter of the "fodder, frost, and
shock"
When the rooter's on the rampage and the knocker's on
the knock;
For a later theme has drawn us where the echoes rise
and fall—
When the bat is on the bingle and the bug is on the
bawl.

CASEY'S REVENGE.

THERE were saddened hearts in Mudville for a week or even more;
There were muttered oaths and curses—every fan in town was sore.
"Just think," said one, "how soft it looked with Casey at the bat,
And then to think he'd go and spring a bush league trick like that!"

All his past fame was forgotten—he was now a hopeless "shine."
They called him "Strike-Out Casey," from the mayor down the line;
And as he came to bat each day his bosom heaved a sigh,
While a look of hopeless fury shone in mighty Casey's eye.

He pondered in the days gone by that he had been their king,
That when he strolled up to the plate they made the welkin ring;
But now his nerve had vanished, for when he heard them hoot
He "fanned" or "popped out" daily, like some minor league recruit.

He soon began to sulk and loaf, his batting eye went lame;
No home runs on the score card now were chalked against his name;

The fans without exception gave the manager no peace,
For one and all kept clamoring for Casey's quick release.

The Mudville squad began to slump, the team was in the air;
Their playing went from bad to worse—nobody seemed to care.
"Back to the woods with Casey!" was the cry from Rooters' Row.
"Get some one who can hit the ball, and let that big dub go!"

The lane is long, some one has said, that never turns again,
And Fate, though fickle, often gives another chance to men;
And Casey smiled; his rugged face no longer wore a frown—
The pitcher who had started all the trouble came to town.

All Mudville had assembled—ten thousand fans had come
To see the twirler who had put big Casey on the bum;
And when he stepped into the box, the multitude went wild;
He doffed his cap in proud disdain, but Casey only smiled.

"Play ball!" the umpire's voice rang out, and then the game began.

But in that throng of thousands there was not a single fan
Who thought that Mudville had a chance, and with their setting sun
Their hopes sank low—the rival team was leading "four to one."

The last half of the ninth came round, with no change in the score;
But when the first man up hit safe, the crowd began to roar;
The din increased, the echo of ten thousand shouts was heard
When the pitcher hit the second and gave "four balls" to the third.

Three men on base—nobody out—three runs to tie the game!
A triple meant the highest niche in Mudville's hall of fame;
But here the rally ended and the gloom was deep as night,
When the fourth one "fouled to catcher" and the fifth "flew out to right."

A dismal groan in chorus came; a scowl was on each face
When Casey walked up, bat in hand, and slowly took his place;
His bloodshot eyes in fury gleamed, his teeth were clenched in hate;
He gave his cap a vicious hook and pounded on the plate.

But fame is fleeting as the wind and glory fades away;
There were no wild and woolly cheers, no glad acclaim
this day;
They hissed and groaned and hooted as they clamored:
"Strike him out!"
But Casey gave no outward sign that he had heard this
shout.

The pitcher smile and cut one loose—across the plate it
sped;
Another hiss, another groan. "Strike one!" the umpire
said.
Zip! Like a shot the second curve broke just below the
knee.
"Strike two!" the umpire roared aloud; but Casey made
no plea.

No roasting for the umpire now—his was as easy lot;
But here the pitcher whirled again—was that a rifle
shot?
A whack, a crack, and out through the space the leather
pellet flew,
A blot against the distant sky, a speck against the blue.

Above the fence in center field in rapid whirling flight
The sphere sailed on—the blot grew dim and then was
lost to sight.
Ten thousand hats were thrown in air, ten thousand
threw a fit,
But no one ever found the ball that mighty Casey hit.

O, somewhere in this favored land dark clouds hide the
sun,

And somewhere bands no longer play and children have
no fun!
And somewhere over blighted lives there hangs a heavy
pall,
But Mudville hearts are happy now, *for Casey hit the
ball.*

THE BUG'S VIEW-POINT.

BEYOND the sleet, across the snows
He did not see the budding rose
That waved its crimson welcome to
An earth of green, a sky of blue,
Nor yet the daffy daffodils
That crowned the valleys and the hills;
The apple blossoms, pink and white,
That drifted into lanes of light;
He did not hear the bluebird sing
Nor yet the south wind whispering
In murmur through the maple trees
That swayed and slanted to the breeze
And harbored on each bending limb
The maker of a woodland hymn—
And yet, like every living thing,
He, too, had drawn his dream of spring.

He saw a gent arrayed in blue
Heave boldly into public view,
And in a fog-horn tenor call
To thousands: "Batter up—play ball!"
He saw a tall guy nod and beck
And then cut one around the neck,
While in a trance the slugger there
Inanely paddled at the air;
He saw the shortstop leave his place
And flag one back of second base
And wing it swiftly on ahead
To where the dashing runner sped;

He saw, before his flashing eye,
The keen outfielder fenceward fly,
And with a mighty effort pull
The drive down with the bases full.

He heard once more the rooters call,
The ringing clash of bat and ball,
The cry of "Belt it on the snout!
Don't try to bunt there, whale it out!"
The groans and curses, cheers and jeers
Like music tinkled in his ears;
The grandstand rocked and roared in strife,
The howling bleachers leaped to life,
As whooping, jeering, shouting, cheering,
Praying, cursing, pleading, fearing,
Stamping, howling, smiling, growling,
Laughing, weeping, snarling, scowling,
Over city, field, and glen
The Bugland Chorus rang again—
For he, like every other thing,
Had drawn his dream of golden spring.

THE COURTSHIP OF A SON OF SWAT.

THEY were seated in the parlor, and the lights were
burning dim—
He was a major leaguer, she a fan, so fair and trim;
But they knew not as he opened up the game by murmuring "Love"
That father was the umpire on the stairway just above.

"I like your form," he led off first; "with me you've
made a hit;
Your curves are good, you've got the speed, and you are
looking fit.
Now if with you, my turtle dove, I make a hit likewise,
Won't you improve my single life and make a sacrifice?"

"I'll promise to support you, dear, with all my skill each
day;
I'll draft a pretty home for you and fix it right away.
If you'll just call the game a tie, I will no longer roam;
And when I slide into the plate, please call me safe at
home."

"First tell me, sir," she pitched at him, "how high you
ranked last fall;
Show me your fielding average and how hard you hit
the ball.
In matrimony's busy league dumb plays are out of place;
I'd like to know the dope before I play too far off base."

"Remember that the game is rough when pay days fail
to come;

He swung like Wagner at his best, a sole-inspiring clout;
The son of swat slid down the steps; the umpire yelled: "You're out."

Sometimes the salary whip is lame, the noodle's on the bum;
And don't forget you'll be reserved for life and held in line,
But promise me you'll never jump your contract, and I'll sign."

He started warning up at once, with victory in his eye,
He shoved a fast one round her neck, the other was waist high.
Just here the umpire butted in. She said: "O, father, please,
There's nothing wrong, for George is only showing me the squeeze!"

The old man gave an irate snort and said: "I'll help the fun
By showing George another play that's called 'the hit and run.'"
He swung like Wagner at his best, a sole-inspiring clout;
The son of swat slid down the steps; the umpire yelled: "You're out!"

THE BUSH LEAGUER'S DREAM.

(From our "Songs of the Spring Recruit.")

I.

THE young recruit stood dreaming where the sultry sun
was beaming,
With the perspiration streaming down his neck;
He had missed four easy chances, which aroused some
angry glances,
And he saw his big league fancies were a wreck;
His work had been erratic, and he heard one mad
fanatic
Yell in tones far from ecstatic: "Chase that cheese!"
Whereupon he drew a vision that was all to the Ely-
sian,
And he spoke with much decision words like these:

Chorus.

"If I could run the bases like Bill Bryan,
If I only had Ted Roosevelt's batting eye,
If I had the reach of Thomas Fortune Ryan,
I'd never let another chance get by;
If I only was as cool as Charley Fairbanks;
Or had control like Harriman has got,
I'd be the diamond daisy, and I'd set the bleachers crazy,
For I'd be the greatest player of the lot."

II.

There had been a dearth of scoring, and the anxious
Bugs were roaring

In the bleachers and imploring for a hit,
Until finally one fellow plucked a triple, ripe and mel-
low,
And the way those fans did bellow in a fit!
Just one little tap would cinch it, just one timely little
pinch hit,
And the contest would be safely on the shelf;
But the bush league phenom madly swung in vain at
three, then sadly
Walked away and murmured softly to himself:

Chorus.

"If I only had a batting eye like Teddy,
If I had the speed of John D. ducking fines,
I'd have a big league job and hold it steady,
For I'd make both Cobb and Wagner look like shines;
If I could only 'steal' (in running bases)
Like all these 'malefactors of great wealth,'
I'd be the diamond daisy, and I'd set the bleachers crazy,
And I wouldn't be here playing for my health."

SPRINGTIME IN THE HISTORY ROOM.

SHE spoke of Alexander as an eminent commander,
And showed 'em how this gentleman was always on the job;
But freckled Mickie Horner, blinking over in the corner,
Dreamed of Cobb.

She praised the late J. Caesar as a keen, artistic geezer
Whose performances in most ways deserved a lasting bonus;
But little Tim O'Grady, though his eyes were on the lady,
Thought of Honus.

She lauded Mr. Hannibal, the chocolate-colored cannibal;
But when she asked young Heinie Schmidt who made the Romans dance,
With his brain-wheels on the whir, Heinie, looking up at her,
Answered: "Chance."

She spoke of Greek and Roman and of horsemen and bowmen,
Of phalanxes and legions in the mediæval game,
Of Goths and Huns and Vandals and such other early scandals
Known to fame.

But young Timothy O'Toole, as he cantered home from
school,
Lost but little time forgetting what he termed "a
bunch of dubs,"
As he doped the playing science of the Pirates, Sox, and
Giants
And the Cubs.

THE HOLD-OUT LEAGUE.

WHAT has become of Bill Wiggins, the old star who passed up the game?
The three-hundred hitter who swore on his oath he would never return to the same?
He is still out of line as he promised, but suffering deeply with pain—
Poor Bill broke a leg when reporting day came in an effort to catch the first train.

Where is Pat Kelly, the slabman, who swore he had pitched his last ball?
Who tore up his contract and said with a roar he "was finished for good and for all."
When the Giants all meet at the depot, in vain Mr. Kelly they seek,
But they find on arriving in Texas that Pat has already been there a week.

"This dope I give out's on the level," said Mike in a hot interview.
"Just make it as strong as the paper will stand. I will never come back; I am through."
But when they arrived at the station, when the train to the training camp led,
They had to tie Mike to a telegraph pole to keep him from running ahead.

There is gloom in the camp of the Pirates—the Giants throw a fit of alarm,

For Matty and Wagner and Tenny have quit to take up
a job on the farm.
But it's queer when you turn to the line-up at the
"Opening Chorus of Bing,"
That the first guys to quit on the diamond each fall are
the first ones at bat in the spring.

THE SONG OF THE BASE HIT.

A TWIST, a whirl, and a sudden jar,
And off from the bat to the field afar—
Off like the shot from a ten-inch gun,
A gray-white streak through the slanting sun
        I soar away
        Through a summer's day
        Where the frantic fielders of the fray,
        With dervish dance
        And anguished glance,
      Come whirling in to cop me;
        But I glide between
        With a mocking mien,
      And there is none to stop me.

A shout, a roar, and a ringing cheer,
And on my way through the atmosphere
I leap to the light where clenched hands grip
As wild eyes watch me fly or skip
        Through open space
        In headlong race,
        As the joy of the ages lights each face
        And pulses jump
        With a vibrant thump
      As the sky reels from the roar,
        And the rafters ring
        With the song I sing
      To the tune of the winning score!

The song I sing is the sweetest song
Or the saddest note to the waiting throng

That the world has known through the ages dim—
With keener lilt than a battle hymn,
  For my refrain
  Brings joy and pain,
  Where lost hopes rise and fond hopes wane,
  And in my path
  Sweeps a city's wrath
 Or a city's wild acclaim,
  And the planet's ring
  With the song I sing—
 The song of a nation's game!

ON THE ROAD TO ROOTERS' ROW.

(Letting Mr. Kipling in, of course, on a bit of the graft.)

I.

In each long-deserted ball park from New York to Tennessee
There's the whisper of an echo wafted forth to you and me;
For the wind calls through the pine trees and the maples, soft and low:
"Come ye back, ye wild Fanatic—come ye back to Rooters' Row."

On the road to Rooters' Row,
In the sunlight's golden glow,
Can't you hear those mad Bugs whooping
As the pitcher fans a foe?
On the road to Rooters' Row,
Where the sad fans wail in woe—
Then a cheer comes up like thunder
When the shortstop lays him low.

II.

When the peanut husks are falling and the "pop" is flowing free,
Where they pound you on the backbone in a massive fit of glee,
Where the "Hit 'er out, you sucker!" greets the batsman true and tried;
Then a boding hush of terror, then a "Slide, you bonehead, slide!"

On the road to Rooters' Row, etc.

III.

O the war whoops from the coachers as they writhe and
dance about!
O the "joshing" of the Sun Gods as they rise up with a
shout!
O the call of "thief" and "pirate" at the Fan Flock's
greatest foe,
As the lordly umpire wanders once again by Rooters'
Row!

On the road to Rooters' Row, etc.

IV.

Ship me somewhere into springtime where a sprinter
starts for "first,"
Where the only one commandment is "To win, or
you're the worst;"
For I feel the fever coming once again to hear the call
Of the vibrant-voiced director and his "Batter up—play
ball!"

On the road to Rooters' Row, etc.

"TILL THE LAST MAN IS OUT."

OLD pal, is the game just a trifle too rough?
  Is the flag of success floating out of your view?
Does the schedule of Life seem too rocky and tough?
  Is the umpire "throwing it into you?"
It may look that way, but fight on just the same,
  Get back at your rivals with "clout for clout;"
Don't think you are beaten and so pull up lame,
  For "the game's never lost till the last man is out."

"Run out every hit," whether hard one or not,
  "Sacrifice" right when it's well up to you;
Don't try to "hammer the ball from the lot,"
  Just "hit where they ain't," and a single will do.
There's many a line-up that came from behind
  When the outlook was gloomy and clouded with doubt;
You'll be in the running if you'll bear in mind:
  "No game's ever lost till the last man is out."

Quite often the "hoodoo will camp on your trail,"
  And the luck break against you with never a stop;
The harder you struggle, the more you will fail
  As you "fumble 'em," "boot 'em," and "let 'em all drop."
But it's all "in the game," so swing on to your pace,
  And don't mind the knocking that's floating about;
It's the finish that counts, not the start of the race,
  And "the game's never lost till the last man is out."

Good fortune may take you along for a day,
  But Fortune is fickle; don't bank on her strong.

"Fast work on the bases" in each scrappy fray,
With "team work and hitting," will take you along.
You can't help your errors, but cut out "dumb plays,"
For those are the miscues that put you to rout;
"Stand up to the plate" and remember always:
"The game's never lost till the last man is out."

L'ENVOI.

When you ponder it over, they're both much the same,
For life, just like baseball, is shrouded in doubt;
And the point in them both is to "play out the game,"
And never give up till "the last man is out."

THE BUSHERS.

(A big advance order is now in for Christy Matthewson's forthcoming volume on baseball; John L. Sullivan is at work upon a romance of the ring, of which he is the hero; Battling Nelson has just closed up a comfortable wad upon his edition of "The Life and Battles of Matthew Battling Nelson.")

WHAT league did Shakespeare ever lead?
That busher Byron had the nerve
To peddle out poetic creed,
Who never batted at a curve.
I'll bet this Dante was a bluff,
And minor leaguer on the side;
For while he wrote a bale of stuff,
His name is not in Spaulding's guide.

What belt did Homer ever win?
Fine chance that dub would have to-day
To cash in on the easy tin
Who never put his man away;
And Milton had the nerve to try
To make a living out of verse,
Who never closed a rival's eye
Or split the big end of a purse.

No wonder in the days of yore
Those ancient artists had no chance
To chew a steak—or that they wore
Big, healthy patches on their pants;
In place of farming out a crop
Of rhyme and meter without flaw,
They should have learned to throw a drop
Or slam a wallop to the jaw.

THE CLIMAX OF FAN JOY.

THERE was cheering in the grandstand when Bill Bradley hit to right,
And the bleachers whooped and clamored in a chorus of delight;
And when the twirler lost control and passed the next two "up,"
The wine of human happiness brimmed swiftly o'er the cup.

The bases full, with two men out, and Larry at the bat.
O, can you wonder that each fan should stand and wave his hat?
Or can you wonder that the yelp should percolate the gloam,
With Larry waiting anxiously to bring the runners home?

The pitcher whirls and cuts one loose—a brawny gent is he—
And, like a cannon shot, it shoots above the batsman's knee;
He swings—and lo! from every throat of that excited crowd
There comes a shriek of fiendish joy—protracted long and loud.

The fans arise and yelp in glee, while hats are thrown in air;
The mighty chorus echoes from the ball yard to the square;

The greatest laugh of all crowns a scrappy game of ball
When a foul-tip cracks the umpire on the knee.

It rumbles down the valley and resounds from peak to
peak,
And leagues away it travels on in one discordant shriek.

They stamp and shout in maddened rout; they joyfully
embrace—
A smile of perfect happiness illumines every face;
Nor does the tumult quickly die, but, in exultant roar,
It gathers volume like the waves which lash the ocean's
shore.

"Then Larry must have made a hit and cleared the
sacks," you say,
"Thus winning with a mighty swat the hard-fought,
brilliant fray!"
No, Larry didn't make a hit; the cause of all this din,
The inshoot caromed off his bat and cracked the
umpire's shin.

SONGS OF SWAT—
"YOU USTER BAT .300."

A ONCE Big Leaguer slid in home at 3 A.M. one morn
With a perfect fielding average in the League of Barleycorn.
He had pulled down fifteen high balls, every one quite warm and hot,
And at every chance presented he was Wagner on the spot.
But as he fumbled at the key his wife was waiting there
With his favorite ash furniture suspended in the air;
And as he tried to curve across she bunted at his head
And slammed a triple on his neck as viciously she said:

Chorus.

"You uster to hit .300—O, your batting was immense!
You uster slam 'em every day against the left field fence;
But now you're in a bush league, for there ain't no guy in sight
Can bat around three hundred, Bo, who bats around all night."

The Leaguer tried to play it safe before she fanned him out.
"I'll make a sacrifice," he cried, "but ease up on that clout;
Hans Wagner never saw the day when he could hit like that.
I only wish that John McGraw could see you swing a bat."

In vain he tried to score a run; in vain he shed each
tear;
In vain he tried to reach his mask and breast protector
gear.
She tagged him all around the room, no matter how
he'd slide,
And rapped out doubles on his back as viciously she
cried:

Chorus.

"You uster to hit .300—O, your batting eye was great!
The pitchers uster to jump the league when you came
to the plate;
But now they've got you faded, for there ain't no guy in
sight
Can bat around three hundred, Bo, who bats around all
night."

THE TEST.

NEVER mind the speed you've got,
Never mind about your curve,
Though it sail around the lot
With a zigzag and a swerve;
How you grip or twist the ball
Enters not upon the scroll;
Here's the answer to it all:
How is your control?

Never mind how hard you swing,
Or the keenness of your eye,
As the pitcher takes a fling
And the pellet whistles by;
With the hard-fought battle done,
Here's the answer to it all:
When a base hit might have won,
Did you hit the ball?

Never mind about the luck,
Or the umpire robbing you—
How the Fates were there to buck
Everything you tried to do;
Cut it out and let it go;
In the Book of Praise or Blame
This is all there is to know:
Did you play the game?

THE LAUGH ON NERO.

AMONG the Coliseum throng King Nero sat him down;
A toga wrapped his shoulder blade, upon his face a frown.
"Ho! turn the tigers loose," he cried, "and bring the lions out!"
At which the massive mob stood up and cheered with mighty shout.

The fiercest lions Numidia had ever grown were there,
The most blood-thirsty Tigerines from Bengal's far-famed lair.
For weeks no food of any sort had been left in their cage
To work each beast into a pitch of gnawing, clawing rage.

Out in the center of the throng the victim took his stand,
A careless smile upon his lips, no weapon in his hand;
He looked serenely on the mob which clamored for his gore,
And faced the tiges with smothered yawns, unmindful of their roar.

The signal given, with a snarl each lion and tiger rushed
Upon their prey, while all around the multitude sat hushed,
While waiting for their victim to be scattered, limb from limb,

But lo, the victim stood his ground, and with a lordly air
He waved each lion and tiger back and gave them glare for glare.

And many Roman coins were bet on what they'd do to
him.

But lo! the victim stood his ground, and with a lordly
air
He waved each lion and tiger back and gave them glare
for glare.
He listened while they growled around and howled at
him a bit;
Then pointed toward the nearest gate and simply
answered, "Git!"

Before that gesture and that look—that voice so cold
and keen—
The growling monsters beat it very quickly from the
scene;
While with a bored and a blasé air, unmindful of his
cup,
The victim took another "chew," and cried, "Next batter
up."

Upon his perch King Nero sat, quite thunderstruck
with awe.
"This is the strangest gent," said he, "that I have ever
saw.
By all the gods of ancient Rome who can this duffer
be?"
"I used to umpire," he replied; "this job was pie for me."

CURFEWED.

FRINGED by clouds, the sun was setting
O'er the hills so far away,
Filling all the land with beauty
At the close of yesterday.
And the straggling rays, descending,
Fell upon all fandom there—
Fans with aching, anguished bosoms,
Fans bowed down in bleak despair.

"Jimmy," said a little newsboy
To a ragged pal near by,
Who sat frowning at the score board
With a teardrop in his eye,
"We ain't got a chance to make it;"
And his face was set and white.
"Orth has got us on the hog train—
Cleveland can't win out to-night."

Every fan from box to bleachers
Sat in silence, sick and sore,
As each inning sped by swiftly
And the Naplets failed to score;
For New York had pounded Otto
Steadily from left to right,
So it looked like easy money
Cleveland wouldn't win that night.

In the meanwhile Orth was puzzling
Every batter on our team;

So the chance to land a victory
  Seemed an empty, idle dream.
Nothing doing in the seventh,
  Till at last above the crowd
New York's brace of luscious tallies
  Hovered like a midnight cloud.

Sitting on his bench, Clark Griffith
  Softly murmured: "Twenty-three,
Skidoo, Larry, to the shadows
  Of the Ancient Apple Tree."
Mr. Orth was smiling blandly,
  With the finish just in sight,
Thinking as he shot one over:
  "Cleveland's out of it to-night."

Two more rounds to make a rally,
  Two more rounds to turn the trick!
Can you wonder for a minute
  Why the cranks were feeling sick?
Not an echo from the grandstand,
  There was dearth of whoops and cheers,
With the ghastly silence broken
  Only by the splashing tears.

"Batter up," said Umpire Connor.
  Larry strode up to the plate
With a bludgeon in his talons,
  While his teeth were clenched in hate.
Bing! Was that another earthquake,
  Or a cyclone in the air?

For the mighty shout that followed
  Must have rumbled through the Square.

Rossman followed and the tumult
  Grew into a maddened shout.
Bing! The racket grew terrific;
  Two on base and no one out.
Jackson next! And hopes long buried
  Rose anew upon the wing.
"Soak her, Jimmy!" shrieked the rooters,
  And the echo answered: "*Bing!*"

Bradley forced, but Bemis singled;
  One had scored, and every sack
Had a sprinter only waiting
  For another welcome crack.
Tighter, tighter grew the tension;
  Stovall went to bat for Hess.
Stovall with his little horseshoe—
  Lucky George? Well, I should guess.

Well, by now you've heard the story
  Of the wild throw Conroy made
When he tagged out Harry Bemis
  And a double play essayed.
Al Orth was a blighted being,
  Griffith's hair turned snowy white;
For, in place of New York winning,
  Cleveland copped the game last night.

THE FAN AND HIS WAY.

THERE was a fan in our town, and he was wondrous wise;
"Aw, hit 'er out!" he'd yell in rage at every sacrifice;
And when some player tried to bunt and got choked off at first,
This wild-eyed fan arose in wrath, and bitterly he cursed:

"Of all the dubs as slow as tubs
I ever saw play ball,
Of all the jokes—the fat-head blokes—
That guy has got the call!
What made him spring a trick like that,
There ain't nobody knows.
Chop out that bunt, you crazy runt,
And slap it on the nose!"

There was a fan in our town, and he was wondrous wise.
The selfsame gent that yelled in rage at every sacrifice;
But when a player lined one out, instead of sacrificing,
And cracked into a double play, the outburst was surprising:

"Of all the fat-heads, far and near,
I ever saw play ball,
Of all the mutts—the brainless butts—
That guy has got the call!
When it gets down to bush league work,
That lobster takes the cake.

Why don't you bunt, you crazy runt,
When that's the play to make?"

There was a fan in our town, and he had wondrous eyes,
And when the umpire called a strike he'd howl in mad surprise;
And on some play at second base, full fifty yards away,
Behind the screen he'd rise in wrath, with sundry things to say:

"What? That man out? Wake up, old scout!
No wonder we lose games!
He had that beat by a dozen feet,
You second Jesse James!"
Of course the umpire, on the spot,
Could not outline the play
Like that wise guy with eagle eye,
Two hundred feet away.

There was a fan in our town—the team won out that night—
He swore by all the ancient gods the bunch was out of sight;
Next day they lost, but what he said was private information,
Or what is technically called "unfit for publication."

"_____! ______! _____!
D____! ______! _____!"
And other phrases which, alas!
I know, beyond a doubt,
Would bring a moral shock if I
Should fill the spaces out.

OVER THE PLATE.

BILL JONES had the speed of a cannon ball;
He could loosen a brick from a three-foot wall.
When he shot one across, it would hurtle by
Too swiftly for even the surest eye.
No one could hit him when he was right,
As no eye could follow the ball's quick flight.
Bill should have starred in a big league rôle,
But he stuck to the "minors"—he lacked control.

Jack Smith had a curve like a loop-the-loop;
It would start for your head with a sudden swoop
And break to your knee with a zigzag wave,
And the league's best batters would roar and rave
At the jump it took and the sudden swerve.
Shades of the Boomerang! What a curve!
But Jack's still doomed to a "bush league" Fate—
He could not "get it across" the plate.

Tom Brown had both the speed and the curves,
A combination which jarred the nerves.
He would steam 'em by till they looked like peas,
And they'd take a jump from your neck to your knees,
From the best to the worst in the league—by Jing!
He had them all in the Phantom Swing,
But he missed the mark of the Truly Great—
Poor Tom, he couldn't locate the plate.

How is it with you, if I may ask?
Have you "got control" of your daily task?
Have you "got control" of your appetite?

Of your temper and tongue in the bitter fight?
Have you "got control" of your brawn and brain?
Or are you laboring all in vain?
It matters not what your daily rôle—
Have you GOT CONTROL? HAVE YOU GOT CONTROL?

It counts not what you may "have," my friend,
When the story is told at the game's far end;
The greatest brawn and the greatest brain
The world has known may be yours in vain.
The man "with control" is the one who mounts,
And it's "how you use what you've got" that counts.
Have you got "the bead?" Are you aiming straight?
How much of your effort "goes over the plate?"

KNOCKING SLANG.

(*Collier's Weekly* and the New York *Tribune* have started a crusade against slang once more, and especially the brand used in detailing ball games.)

NIX on the slang; chop out the stuff;
   That ain't no way to pass the dope out.
Crawl easy on this line of guff
   And push it for a gentle slope out;
Don't make the English spiel a joke
   By crabbing up the conversation;
Give it a chance correctly spoke
   Without some wise mutt's explanation.

If there is one thing puts the punk
   Kibosh upon me, it's the geezer
Who's always spieling out some junk
   And running in some funny wheezer;
Who jams in with a bunch of talk
   That listens like it had a cancer,
Until somebody calls a balk
   And grabs a chart to pick the answer.

Why ain't the old spiel good enough
   That's lined out in the dictionary,
That we must draw this cross-fire guff
   To which no sane gazabe is jerry?
I'll take mine in the simple buzz
   When Noah Webster led the batting.
He had these slangsters on the buzz
   When it came down to big league chatting.

Nix on this slang; it's on the blink,
   And my remarks are here emphatic.
The geek who slings it through the ink
   Has beetles in his bush league attic.
Let's slip in on the Big Revive
   For scholarly and classic diction.
Come on, you mutts now, with the dive
   And do a Brodie at this fiction.

THE REAL SPRINGTIME.

I DO not care about the spring
Of which the high-browed poets sing—
Of vines, where budding blossoms cling,
And all that sort of blooming thing.
I care not for the triolet
Which boosts the early violet,
Nor buzzing bees, nor budding trees,
Now scented stuff upon the breeze;
The bard who brays of meadows green
To me is balmy in the bean.

I do not care about the spring,
Of happy larks upon the wing,
Of mocking birds that rise and sing,
And all that fuzzy sort of thing;
I care not for the "April snow,"
Of white bloom wafted to and fro,
"The sunlit weather," purple heather,
Lovers-down-the-lane-together;
The dope who draws this brand of throb
To me is knotty in the knob.

But hail—thrice hail—the golden spring
Which ushers in the spitball "fling;"
The echo of the three-base "bing."
Which makes the Bugland welkin ring;
The shout across the Great Divide
Of "Slide, you bonehead lobster, slide!"

The mighty roar that sings the score,
The chance to lap the umpire's gore;
T'ell with your mocking bird's spring call—
Give me the melody, "Play Ball."

THE RAVEN UP-TO-DATE.

LAST night while I pondered dreary, grouchy, sore, and limp and leary,
O'er the dope in my apartments, far up on the thirteenth floor;
As I nodded, nearly napping, suddenly there came a tapping,
As of some one gently rapping, rapping at my chamber door.
"'Tis some bill collector," thought I, "rapping at my chamber door—
Only that and nothing more."

Ah, distinctly I remember, I was thinking of September,
And the finish of the league race—what the future had in store;
And I started prophesying where the pennant would be flying,
Till at last I gave up trying, feeling very sad and sore,
For the dope was so uncertain that I gave up sad and sore,
Grumbling slowly: "Nevermore."

As I sat there, nearly bug house, longing for a near-by jug house,
Once again I heard the tapping, tapping at my chamber door;
So I oped it, shrinking craven, wishing for some happy haven,

When, behold! there flapped a Raven, stalking in across the floor—
Stalking Edgar Allen Poeish, right across my rugless floor.
Ach, du Leiber! I was sore.

"Raven!" cried I, "why the devil have you come here? On the level,
I thought Mr. Poe had written you would enter nevermore.
What has brought you, you intriguer, with that look so keen and eager?
Speak up there, you old bush leaguer; why have you returned, you bore?
State your trouble and then skip, sir; leave me quickly, I implore!"
Quoth the Rave: "What's the score?"

A DAY IN THE BLEACHERS.

(Being a true chronicle of the comments offered by Mike the Bite as the game was in progress, wedged into verse.)

I.

W'AT'S dat? A *ball!* Aw, say, yer make me weary.
Why don't yer call dem strikes, you Jesse James?
No wonder dat the ball club's lookin' leery,
Wid blind men on de job empirin' games.
I'm glad I left my watch at home, you pirate,
When I see de style wot goes wit' you to-day.
Why, dat Ali Baba geezer was a fat-head bush league teaser
When it gits down to de scientific way.

II.

Wake up, you fathead! Take a wallop at it!
Swing at dem balls wot slopes across de plate!
Don't stand dere like a blear-eyed mummy—bat it!
Dis ain't no place to dream, you drunken skate.
T'ree strikes and out, and still yer're on de pay roll.
I only wisht I owned dis baseball club;
An' de first t'ing dat I'd do would be to hitch a can to you
'Bout de size of Lockout Mountain, Mr. Dub.

III.

Say, dat guy playin' second is a dandy.
Did yer pipe him block dat bingle on de bound?

He's got Ted Roosevelt double-crossed fur candy
    When it comes to swingin' hard and coverin' ground;
But de mutt wot went and booted dat last roller—
    He'd duck to-night if I but had my wish.
In my time I t'ink I've seen a bunch o' dubs some punk-
        erino,
    But dat feller couldn't ketch contagious fish!

A WARNING.

MAKERS of bonnets the women wear,
   Molders of fashion, whoe'er ye be,
Drear is the curse of my daily prayer,
   Deep is the hatred I have for thee.
This is the warning I fling afar:
   "Mold 'em more on a smaller plan.
Chop off a couple of yards of 'spar,'
   Or beware the wrath of an angry fan."

Yesteryear to the game I went,
   Daily the pilgrimage I made.
O what a waste of coin I spent,
   Wondering there how the game was played!
Was it a hit or an error raw?
   Was it a stolen base or score?
I peered in vain, but I only saw
   A hat that was nine feet wide or more!

Back to the park this spring I passed,
   Knowing the old styles out of date.
"Now," I thought, "I shall get at last
   A look once more at the old 'home plate.'"
Was it a hit or fielding flaw?
   Why the deuce did the bleachers roar?
In vain I looked, but I only saw
   A hat that was nine feet high or more!

Makers of bonnets the women wear,
   Molders of fashion, whoe'er ye be,

In vain I looked, but I only saw
A hat that was nine feet high or more!

A Warning.

Drear is the curse of my daily prayer,
   Deep is the hatred I have for thee.
This is the warning I hurl to-day:
   "Cut on a narrower, shorter plan;
Chop off a couple of yards each way,
   Or beware the wrath of a maddened fan."

OUT ON THE LINES.

It isn't so much, "Did you make a hit?" but, "How did you swing at the ball?"
Did you go up to bat with your nerve all gone and never half try at all?
Did your heart beat strong? Were your eye gleams bright? Did you swing as it cut the plate?
Or did you stand in a listless way and hit at the ball too late?

It isn't so much, "Did you score a run?" but, "How did you act on base?"
Did you run it out at the crack of the bat with a rattling, dashing pace?
Did you look for a chance to steal a bag? Did you score by your own keen wit?
Or did you get all the way around on another fellow's hit?

It isn't so much, "Did you win the game?" but, "How did you play, old scout?"
Did you give 'em a fight to the bitter end and scrap till the last was out?
Did you let 'em know they were in a game? Did you always come back strong?
Or did you loaf when the game seemed lost, and quit when the "break" went wrong?

ON MEMORY'S WALL.

OF all the horrible pictures
That hang on memory's wall,
Is one of a certain ball game
That seemeth the worst of all;
Not for the money wasted,
Counting the coin it cost;
Not that the umpire robbed us,
Not that the home team lost;
Not that the shortstop fumbled
Four balls, while I madly cursed,
Nor the catcher caught like a lobster—
It seemeth to me the worst.

I once had a little sweetheart
With eyes that were deep and dark;
Unto that game I took her
Into the baseball park.
Light as the down of thistles,
The fielders chased the ball;
Loud as the roar of tempests
Followed the rooters' call;
And I heard my heart beat loudly
As our star man came to bat,
When my little sweetheart murmured:
"Say, *look* at that woman's hat!"

Loudly the base hit rattled,
Bringing the tieing score;
Wildly the crowd upstarted,
Yelping a mighty roar;

Softly there came the whisper,
  Ending my joyous fit:
"Why is that poor man running?
  What is a three-base hit?"
Therefore of all the pictures
  That hang on memory's wall,
That one of a certain ball game
  It seemeth the worst of all.

THE GAME.

LET'S play it out—this little game called Life,
  Where we are listed for so brief a spell;
Not just to win, amid the tumult rife,
  Or where acclaim and gay applauses swell;
Not just to conquer where some one must lose,
  Or reach the goal, whatever be the cost:
For there are other, better ways to choose,
  Though in the end the battle may be lost.

Let's play it out, as if it were a sport
  Wherein the game is better than the goal,
And never mind the detailed "score's" report
  Of errors made, if each with dauntless soul
But stick it out until the day is done,
  Not wasting fairness, for success or fame,
So when the battle has been lost or won
  The world at least can say: "He played the Game."

Let's play it out—this little game called Work,
  Or War or Love or what part each may draw;
Play like a man who scorns to quit or shirk
  Because the break may carry some deep flaw;
Nor simply holding that the goal is all
  That keeps the player in the contest staying;
But stick it out from curtain rise to fall,
  As if the game itself were worth the playing.

MUDVILLE'S FATE.

(Being No. 3 of the Casey series, depicting the sad finish of Mudville after the celebrated Son of Swat put the township on the blink by whiffing in the championship game, thus wiping out all interest in a hitherto thriving baseball center. The pathetic fate of Mudville afterwards is only equaled by that of the "Deserted Village," so aptly doped out by the late O. Goldsmith, "real" poet.)

I WANDERED back to Mudville, Tom, where you and I were boys,
And where we drew in days gone by our fill of childish joys;
Alas! the town's deserted now, and only rank weeks grow
Where mighty Casey fanned the air just twenty years ago.

Remember Billy Woodson's place, where, in the evening's shade,
The bunch would gather and discuss the home runs Casey made?
Dog fennel now grows thick around that "joint" we used to know,
Before old Casey whiffed the breeze some twenty years ago.

The grandstand, too, has been torn down; no bleachers met my gaze
Where you and I were wont to sit in happy bygone days;

The peanuts which we fumbled there have sprouted in
a row
Where mighty Casey swung in vain just twenty years
ago.

O how we used to cheer him, Tom, each time he came
to bat!
And how we held our breath in awe when on the plate
he spat;
And when he landed on the ball, how loud we yelped!
But O
How loud we cursed when he struck out some twenty
years ago!

The diamond is a corn patch now; the outfield's over-
grown
With pumpkin vines and weedy plots; the rooters all
have flown—
They couldn't bear to live on there, for nothing was the
same
Where they had been so happy once before that fatal
game.

The village band disbanded soon; the mayor, too,
resigned.
The council even jumped its graft, and in seclusion
pined;
The marshal caught the next train out, and those we
used to know
Began to leave in flocks and droves some twenty years
ago.

For after Casey fanned that day the citizens all left,
And one by one they sought new lands, heartbroken and bereft;
The joyous shout no more rang out of children at their play;
The village blacksmith closed his shop; the druggist moved away.

Alas for Mudville's vanished pomp when mighty Casey reigned!
Her grandeur has departed now; her glory's long since waned.
Her place upon the map is lost, and no one seems to care
A whit about the old town now since Casey biffed the air.

A TOAST WORTH WHILE.

YE may drink if ye will to the star of renown
   Who is listed far over the mass,
Who has planted his name on the hallway of fame
   At a height which no other can pass.
I will take off my hat to a player like that—
   He is worthy of plaudits, I know—
And none can refuse to extend him his dues,
   And we'll bow down to him in a row.

But come; fill you glasses, my lads and my lasses—
A toast as the wine drops run;
"And here's to the fellow who plays the game and sticks
      till the game is done."

Ye may drink, if ye will, to the brilliant brigade
   And the hair-raising chances they take;
To their wonderful stops and their fast-breaking drops,
   And the one-handed catches they make.
They are worthy of fame, for they light up the game,
   And it's right that their luster should grow;
And none can refuse to extend them their dues,
   And we'll bow down to them in a row.

Then, ho! fill your glasses, my lads and my lasses—
A toast as the red drops run:
"And here's to the fellow who plays the game and sticks
      till the game is done."

It doesn't count much at the tale's far end
   Whether victory cometh or not,

If but early and late we will stand to the plate,
  And give 'em the best we have got;
If we'll keep up the fight till the end is in sight
  And never give up, though we tire—
Although out of breath, we'll "be in at the death"
With a pretty fair lead at the wire.

So up with your glasses, my lads and my lasses—
A toast as the wine drops run:
"And here's to the fellow who plays the game and sticks
    till the game is done."

THE CHAMPS OF THE ALLEY LEAGUE.

JUST at this time every season, when the sun beats down on the street;
When the breath of another springtime comes up with its fragrance sweet;
When the winter league race is over, and the clans of a new campaign
Are camped in the fields of Dixie, cheered on by the fan refrain;
As they talk of a coming pennant or speak of an all-star team
My fancy flies on the south wind, on the crest of an old, old dream,
Back where the eye gleamed brightly, where the soul knew no fatigue,
When I was one of "The Ragged Stars," the champs of the Alley League.

I hear that the "fever is rising," that "the great fan flock once more
Is ready to sit in the bleachers and cheer for the winning score;"
They speak of a "coming wonder," they talk of a "flag to fly,"
They whisper the thrilling story of "Mike and his batting eye;"
But out from the mad fanatics my fancy wanders free
From the hopes of a glad to-morrow to the land of the used-to-be,

Far from the "spit-ball" gossip, far from "McGraw's intrigue,"
Where I "played first" on "The Ragged Stars," the champs of the Alley League.

And what is the mighty Wagner to Mickey, "the Human Slat,"
Who batted around "eight hundred," with a broomstick for a bat?
Where is the "big league gameness" of stars they have set on thrones
To "Johnny the Jew," who tied the score with a slide over cobblestones?
"Matthewson's curves are a mystery," "Walsh is a wonder, too,"
But Pat Maguire set the "strike-out" mark with a pellet of "yarn and glue;"
Boast of your Chance and Jennings, winners of keen intrigue;
But they never stacked up with "The Ragged Stars," the champs of the Alley League.

Just at this time every season, when the March sun warms the town;
When the little green leaves peep shyly from the stark, bare limbs of brown;
When the voice of the rooter rises in the roll of a rippling cheer,
The winds of another springtime blow back from another year.
The cry of the barefoot legions, the shouts of the tattered host

As twinkling feet raced madly in a dash for the tele-
phone post,
To a wagon wheel "for second base," with never a touch
of fatigue,
When I was one of "The Ragged Stars," the champs of
the Alley League.

THE MAN WHO PLAYED WITH ANSON ON THE OLD CHICAGO TEAM.

(A case parallel to Eugene Field's account of "The Man Who Worked with Dana on the Noo York *Sun*.")

THAR showed up out in Mudville in the spring of '83
A feller evidently just recoverin' from a spree.
He said his name was Casey, and he wuz a sight to view
As he walked into the ball park, and inquired for work to do.
Thar wuzn't any openin', for you should understand
That wuz the time when Mudville had a bunch of stars on hand;
But the stranger lingered, tellin' Mickey Nolan and the rest
What an all-fired battin' av'rage he possessed when at his best,
Till finally he stated, quite by chance, as it would seem,
That he had played with Anson on the old Chicago team.

Wal, that was quite another thing; we owned that any cuss
Who'd played with old Pop Anson must be good enough for us;
So we took Casey at his word and signed him while we could,
Well knowin' if we didn't that some other ball club would,

For Kankakee wuz lookin' round for people that could
play,
And Pikeville wouldn't overlook this feller any day;
And we give him quite a contract, tho' it made the
others swear,
Sayin' we had done 'em dirty and it wuzn't on the
square;
But we laid back and cackled, for the pennant warn't no
dream
With the man who'd played with Anson on the old
Chicago team.

It made our eyeballs nigh pop out and pop back in
again
To hear that Casey tellin' of old Anson and his
men;
Why home runs wuz so common that nobody waved a
hat,
With Williamson, King Kelly, or Fred Pfeffer at the
bat;
A man who didn't hit above .500 couldn't stick
With that old bunch, for Anson would release him
mighty quick;
They handled ground balls with their teeth and often
shut their eyes
While in the act of pullin' down the longest, hardest
flies;
And after all the "fannin' bees" each night we used to
dream
Of the man who played with Anson on the old Chicago
team.

But somehow this feller Casey never felt like goin' in;
He spent his time at Wilson's shakin' poker dice for
gin.
Whenever he wuz needed he wuz always sure to shirk,
Remarkin' he would have to wait before he started
work.
If any other gent had loafed the way he used to do,
We'd have fined him fifty dollars every day, and
benched him too;
But you see the fans respected him and backed him to
the last
On account of his connections with the diamond in the
past,
For no one felt like knockin' or handin' out a call
To the man who'd played on Anson's team, the greatest
of 'em all.

Wal, finally the climax came—the big test of the year—
And the fans wuz there in bunches from the country far
and near,
Especially attracted by the statement made that day
That, having rounded into shape, big Casey wuz to
play.
The other nine wuz lookin' kinder worried and upset,
And they wouldn't even listen to an even-money bet.
We kidded 'em and joshed 'em, but no wagerin' wuz
done,
Till at last they placed a thousand at the odds of ten to
one;
But even at these odds it looked an easy-money
scheme,

With the man who'd played with Anson on the old
Chicago team.

But Casey never drew a chance to shine in any way;
They handed him a base on balls without the least
delay;
The pitcher didn't seem to care to put one over straight
While the man who'd played with Anson was a-standin'
at the plate.
He only had one fly in left, which bounded off his head
(It seems the sun was shinin' in his countenance, he
said);
And so the people waited in much anger and suspense
For Casey's opportunity to drive one through the fence;
And it came—O yes—it landed with a nauseating rap
For the man who'd played with Anson, and referred to
him as "Cap."

Old Mudville was a run behind when that last inning
came;
The bases full and two wuz out—a hit would win the
game.
"He's got to put it over now," each rooter waved his hat,
And shouted in delirium as Casey stepped to bat.
The first two inshoots jumped across the center of the
plate,
As Mr. Anson's college chum found out a bit too late;
The next looked good and Casey swung—there came a
mighty crack—
But the noise originated from the spine in Casey's
back.

In reaching for that outshoot he had wrenched the
spinal beam
Of the man who played with Anson on the old Chicago
team.

. . . .

That night we wired Anson to discover if he knew
A man by name of Casey, as we felt we ought to do;
And when the answer came next day it stirred up quite
a fuss:
"Yes, I remember Casey well—he carried bats for us."

We hunted for him quite a spell, but he had gone away,
Else the daisies would be bloomin' over his remains to-
day.
But if you land in Mudville on the lookout for some
fun,
Don't ever mention Casey's name unless you wear a
gun.

THE RECORD.

WHEN the game is done
 And the players creep,
One by one,
 To the League of Sleep,
Deep in the night
 They may not know
The way of the fight,
 The fate of the foe;
And the cheer that passed
 From applauding bands
Is stilled at last—
 But the record stands.

The base hits made,
 And the errors wrought;
How the game was played,
 How the fight was fought;
Though the game be done
 Where the night is deep
And one by one
 From the field they creep;
Their day has passed
 Through the twilight gates,
But the scroll is cast
 And the record waits.

"THE MAJOR LEAGUER'S DAUGHTER;" OR, "THE TURNING OF THE TIDE."

(Up to the hour of going to press the music of this soon-to-be popular ballad had not been written. The sport department office boy was out at the time, while the janitor was busy; so any who peruse it must compose their own music to the selection.)

THEY were seated in the parlor, where the gas was burning low.
And he held her little paw within his own;
He looked at her and whispered: "Mame, you know I love you so;
You've made more hits with me than Fielder Stone,
Your curves look awful good to me, your speed is just my style."
But here he stopped and sadly bowed his head;
The decision was against him, he was out about a mile,
When unto him these cruel words she said:

Chorus.

"I am the only daughter of a major league phenom,
While you are but an unknown bush league bloke.
My old man hits .300 almost every season, Tom;
While they tell me that your average is a joke.
Some day when you are drafted or you have a batting eye,
I may listen to the words you have to say;
But until you show the goods, take a hike back to the woods,
For there's nothing doing here for you to-day—day—day!"

The years went by and Tom improved; his work began
to shine,
His batting and his fielding were immense.
His average jumped from .083 around .449,
While every day he splintered up some fence.
But in the meantime Mame's old man began to lose his
eye;
They canned him when his salary whip went dead.
So Tom, he passed her up for good, and now she won-
ders why
Them cruel words unto him once she said:

Chorus.

"I am the only daughter of a major league phenom,"
etc.

So Tom, he passed her up for good, and now she wonders
why
Them cruel words unto him once she said.

PEN SNAPSHOT OF THE BRITISH FAN.

(Baseball is making a great hit in England. But even the exciting American game hasn't been strenuous enough to arouse the lethargic Briton from his stolidness. The most exciting plays bring forth only faint applause, such as "Jolly well tried for, old chap."—*Item from Sportman's Review.*)

FOR eight fleeting innings the Warwickshire Browns
Had battled like fiends with the Berkshire brigade;
The grandstand was crowded by fans from the towns
All around who had come out to see the game played.

The hitting and fielding were simply immense,
No snappier game anywhere could be found;
They doubled and tripled and dented the fence,
While one-handed pick-ups were pulled off each round.

With the home team at bat, some performer of brawn
Scored three with a triple—a terrible smash;
His lordship remarked as he stifled a yawn,
"Bloody clever, old chap," and then twirled his mustache.

This swat put the Warwickshire bunch in the lead;
But when the ninth came, every Berkshire fought hard,
And five of them scored in the hour of need
By clouting the leather all over the yard.

In the last of the tenth, four runs to the bad,
 The first home man up made a hurricane swipe;
He tripled to center. "That wasn't half bad,
 Doncher know," said a rooter while puffing his pipe.

Then followed a double that whistled to right;
 Two yeomen, applauding, were chased from the park;
The score was soon tied up with victory in sight.
 "Bah Jove," murmured one, "what a deuce of a lark!"

ON THE COACHING LINE.

GET in the game! Smoke up, old scout!
 We've got to win this scrap to-day.
Take any chance, for two are out;
 Get on your toes and watch the play.
Three balls—wow! wow! I guess he walks.
 Come back, come back; you ain't so lame.
Say there, you thickhead; watch them balks,
 Get in the game; get in the game!

Get in the game, there—at the bat.
 Just pick out one that suits your eye.
I guess those benders don't look fat.
 Don't let a strike like *that* go by!
Just watch 'em over—make 'em ride.
 A hit! A hit! It's all the same,
You'll beat it; slide, you lobster, *slide!*
 Get in the game, get in the game!

Get in the game, no matter which,
 Nor where, nor when, nor who you are.
The slogan rings at lofty pitch
 From inland town to harbor bar,
From lowly surf to ruling kings,
 If you would carve a laureled name,
The distaff of the epoch sings:
 "Get in the game! Get in the game!"

Get in the game, you merchants and
 You lawyers, doctors, preachers too;

You workmen who compose the band
With countless duties yet to do;
You leaders who must head the line,
One dumb play may bring lifelong shame;
Watch every signal, every sign.
Get in the game! Get in the game!

Get in the game—this age is live,
And loafers have no part to play.
If you would win, if you would thrive,
"Keep on your toes" in every fray;
And if you rise or if you fall,
It matters not—the Road to Fame
But echoes with the world-wide call:
"Get in the game! Get in the game!"

THE GOODS.

HERE'S to the guy that delivers the goods—
Gent from the city or geek from the woods;
Hillside or valley, mountain or plain,
Sunshine or shadow or starlight or rain—
Any old time or condition or place;
Taking it easy or rough-house to face,
But putting it over and calling the bluff—
Here's looking—the guy who delivers the stuff.

Here's to the guy that delivers—and, say,
Chop out that dope on the luck of the day;
Fate took a wallop and slipped you the quid?
Well, wotthehell do we care if it did?
That ain't the tip we are looking for here.
Bend down a minute and lend us an ear,
Geek from the brushes or guy from the town:
Did you deliver? Or did you fall down?

THE WINTER LEAGUE WONDER.

THOUGH I've never won a pennant in the race that
starts each spring,
And the finish every autumn finds me muchly to the
"punk;"
Though through June, July, and August you can hear
the anvils ring
As the critics in a body dub my team a bunch of
"junk,"
You have got to hand it to me on a silver platter when
The summer scramble's over. Though some other
mogul wins,
I'm the one and only wonder of the "coming season"
then
When the last *real* game is over and the winter
league begins.

Though each October finds me under every rival's heel,
Twenty games behind the others, do I stop and shed
a tear?
Not upon your uncle's portrait. I begin right off the reel
Lining up my winter legions for a "sure first next
year."
I admit "the luck broke badly" and the "umpires
crimped my chance,"
I confess to "injured players" and a few less minor
sins;
Then I jump out in the open and I do a pennant dance,
When the last *real* game is over and the winter
league begins.

The pitchers I have gathered when the snow begins to
fall
Are the wonders of the nation—every one's a Hurling King;
And my outfield—Holy Whiskers!—how that bunch
can hit the ball
When they walk up with the willow from October
unto spring!
Every player on my pay roll is a star of purest ray,
Till they reach the field of battle, where they're
slower on their "pins"
Than a stream of cold molasses, and my phenoms fade
away—
But you've got to hand it to me when the winter
league begins.

A TIP TO THE FAN FLOCK.

DID you ever have the feeling you were "all in," down, and out,
As of mud upon your skylight, or your brain pan had the gout?
When you sauntered to your office in a semi-hearted way
And earned about one-seventh of your wage or daily pay?
When your energy had left you and your dizzy dome would throb
As you spent the day in yawning or four-flushing on your job?
Well, you have if you are human; so while out among the crowd
In the grandstand or the bleachers, shouting curses long and hard
At some "blot" or costly bobble, let the old dope trickle through
That perhaps the second baseman has the same old feeling too.

While sparring with the cash book or the ledger in your den,
Don't you feel a brain-storm blowing in your noodle now and then?
When the numbers dance around you, while you're ripping, raving mad
That the pesky, peevish figures of the column fail to add?

A Tip to the Fan Flock.

When your orbs feel dry and blinky, and the harder
  that you look,
All the more the figures jumble on the pages of your
  book?
It's a cinch you've had the feeling; so before you seek
  the gore
Of some indicator wielder whose decisions blocked a
  score,
Stop and figure for a second; let the old dope trickle
  through
That the umpire is entitled to his little off-day too.

AS THE GAME "BREAKS."

MULLIGAN "catches the ball on the snout;"
It's just where he likes it; he smashes it out.
Biff—on the trade-mark—it whirls like a shot;
They're yelling and cheering all over the lot.
A shout, then a groan from the well-crowded stands;
The drive travels straight to the outfielder's hands.
Two feet to the left or two feet to the right
And Mulligan's swat would have captured the fight.
Just a matter of inches from out of the line
Changed him from a "star" to a "mutt" and a "shine."
Just two stingy feet—aye, there is the rub—
He didn't hit safe, so they called him a dub.

Pat Flaherty gets one that isn't his kind,
But he closes his orbs and he swings at it blind.
'Twas a weak-sister swat and not one-half as stout
As the one which poor Mulligan "slammed on the
snout."
Yet the bleachers arose with a yelp and a screech
As it twisted just out of an infielder's reach.
It broke up the game, and yet only two feet
Closer in and the tap would have been easy meat;
Just a matter of inches—a bit farther down—
Changed him from a "dub" to a "star" of renown;
Just two pesky feet, but it ended the game,
So they plastered a new-made cigar with his name.

You'll find it the same upon life's massive chart—
The "star" and the "dub" are but inches apart.

As the Game "Breaks."

One smashes out hard, but his drive never lands,
As it travels direct to another one's hands.
The next fellow's effort is puny and tame,
But it hits the right spot and so gathers him fame.
It's the lore of the age from the centuries brought:
"The bunt may roll safe, while the hard smash is
caught."
You may strive twice as hard for the rich prize at stake,
But the fellow that wins is the one "with the break."

THE GRAND OLD WINTER LEAGUE.

HERE'S to the league where they all hit three hundred;
Here's to the league where they all bag the flag;
Here's to the wonderful, mighty, and thunderful
Swat of the artist who's springing the gag—
Springing the gag while the old stove is roaring,
Spieling of games that he won in the pinch;
Fence-breaking hammerer, clean-'em-up slammerer,
Where every pitcher he faced was a cinch.

Here's to the league where they've all cinched the pennant—
Cinched with a line-up that's keen on the job;
Where in the bingtime of oncoming springtime
Every guy signed is a "second Ty Cobb."
Hail to the Wagners and dashing young Matthewsons—
There with the speed and the curves and control;
Swift-footed, heady, keen-eyed, and steady,
Already sewing the flag to the pole.

Here's to the league where the hapless tail-ender
Rises each year to the crest of the game;
Where there is never an artist unclever,
Never a star that is injured or lame;
Where for a spell all the umpires are honest,
Where every mogul has shown keen intrigue;
Hip for the dope from the circuit of hope,
Hail to the glorious Typewriter League!

THE SLIDE OF PAUL REVERE.

LISTEN, fanatics, and you shall hear
Of the midnight slide of Paul Revere;
  How he scored from first on an outfield drive
  By a dashing sprint and a headlong dive—
'Twas the greatest play pulled off that year.

Now the home of poets and potted beans,
Of Emersonian ways and means
In baseball epic has oft been sung
Since the days of Criger and old Cy Young;
But not even fleet, deer-footed Bay
Could have pulled off any such fancy play
As the slide of P. Revere, which won
The famous battle of Lexington.

The Yanks and the British were booked that trip
In a scrap for the New World championship;
But the British landed a bit too late,
So the game didn't open till half past eight,
And Paul Revere was dreaming away
When the umpire issued his call for play.

On, on they fought, 'neath the Boston moon,
As the British figured, "Not yet, but soon;"
For the odds were against the Yanks that night,
With Paul Revere blocked away from the fight
And the grandstand gathering groaned in woe,
While a sad wail bubbled from Rooters' Row.

But wait! Hist! Hearken! And likewise hark!
What means that galloping near the park?
What means that cry of a man dead sore?
"Am I too late? Say, what's the score?"
And echo answered both far and near,
As the rooters shouted: "There's Paul Revere!"

O how sweetly that moon did shine
When P. Revere took the coaching line!
He woke up the grandstand from its trance
And made the bleachers get up and dance;
He joshed the British with robust shout
Until they booted the ball about.
He whooped and he clamored all over the lot,
Till the score was tied in a Gordian knot.

Now, in this part of the "Dope Recooked"
Are the facts which history overlooked—
How Paul Revere came to bat that night
And suddenly ended the long-drawn fight;
How he singled to center, and then straightway
Dashed on to second like Harry Bay;
Kept traveling on, with the speed of a bird,
Till he whizzed like a meteor, rounding third.
"Hold back, you lobster!" but all in vain
The coachers shouted in tones of pain;
For Paul kept on with a swinging stride,
And he hit the ground when they hollered: "Slide!"

Spectacular plays may come and go
In the hurry of Time's swift ebb and flow;

But never again will there be one
Like the first American "hit and run."
And as long as the old game lasts you'll hear
Of the midnight slide of P. Revere.

THE ANNUAL RETURN.

ONE by one they're drifting back—
Hank McGee to Hackensack;
Pat Maguire, the world-famed "spitter;"
Mike the Bite, "three-hundred" hitter;
Jim and Ed and Bill and Jack.
One by one they're drifting back,
With their curves, their keen intrigue,
To the swift Grass Cutter's League.

One by one they leave and go
Back again to Kokomo,
Kankakee and Rural Dell,
Where they cast a mystic spell
On the "scouts" who touted them,
Each a "human diadem,"
In a serried line return
With their "curves and speed to burn."

One by one they fade away
To the fragrant, uncut hay.
"Second Wagners," "second Cobbs"
Back upon their old-time jobs
In the Fried Ham Circuit where
They were stars, with some to spare;
Where they played with famed eclat*
In the field and at the bat.

---

*As in "cat."

The Annual Return.

One by one they file back home
To the sweet scent of the loam;
Yet but one brief month ago
They were "making Walsh look slow"—
Each, the phenom of the age,
Flashed upon the sporting age
As the "greatest of them all"
When it came to playing ball.

Pounding on the beaten track—
Hank McGee to Hackensack,
Pat Maguire to Kankakee
Mike to "Sunny Tennessee"—
In a serried line return,
With their "curves and speed to burn,"
Batting eyes and keen intrigue,
To the swift Grass Cutter's League.

IN THE GOOD OLD WINTER TIME.

(Old, but to the point. As sung by the fan chorus around many circuits.)

I.

An old fan sat one day at a table, small and round,
Drinking every kind of liquid which in that place could be found.
He had forty-seven chances, and he never fumbled one,
Catching sixteen sparkling high balls ere he scored his first home run.

While sitting at that table he began to read the dope,
Which depicted every manager in front up Pennant Slope;
But soon in dreamy fancy from the page he turned away,
And to the near-by barkeep these idle words did say:

Chorus.

"In the good old winter time, the good old winter time,
How swiftly from the bottom all the tail-end people climb.
They call each new recruit a 'peach,' although he is a 'lime.'
O how they nature-fake us in the good old winter time!"

II.

The months rolled by and spring had come, and there on Rooters' Row

The same fan sat with eyes ablaze and ruddy cheeks
aglow.
He saw the "Second Wagner" strike out four times in
one game,
While seven ghastly errors were chalked up against his
name.
He saw the "sterling pitcher" who had "starred" at
"Rural Falls,"
Yield nineteen massive bingles and a dozen base on
balls,
And then above the battle and the rattle of the fray
He softly hummed the chorus of that far-gone winter
day:

Chorus.

"In the good old winter time, the good old winter time,
How swiftly from the bottom all the tail-end people
climb.
By summer almost every 'peach' turns out to be a 'lime.'
O how they nature-fake us in the good old winter
time!"

AFTER THE GAME.

NOW that the hard-fought day is ended,
   With laurels for the favored few;
The cheering and the jeering blended
   In praise or blame that may be due;
Now that the score has been completed,
   Beyond the shallow depths of fame,
Among both Victors and Defeated
   We'll turn to those who played the game.

Not in the losing or the winning,
   Success nor failure for the day;
But from the battle's first beginning
   We'll take their work up, play by play.
How well they tried! how they stood ready!
   Beyond the world crowd's narrow sight
We'll lift our glasses, bravely, steady,
   And drink to those who fought the fight.

The game is done, the fight completed,
   What matters now who reached the goal?
Alike the Victor and Defeated
   Wait for the final scorer's scroll;
And those who look may read the story
   Of star by star against each name,
Set over those with world-won glory,
   The list of those who played the game.

ON ROOTERS' ROW.

I.

WE got a swell chance now to cop wid dat guy at de bat;
Why, say, dat hobo couldn't hit de ball yard wid his hat.
If he was in a steamboat and it blew up in a wreck,
He couldn't hit de water if he tumbled off de deck;
I've paid me month's rent four times since he stung one on de snout,
And what I'm sayin' to you is dat's slumpin' some, old scout.
Two runs to tie, de bases choked; we get 'em to de mat,
And den a piece of cheese like him comes wobblin' to de bat.

Bing! On de nose—O wow! O wow! Beyond de fielder's mitt.
Say, where's de bloomin' guy wot said dat lobster couldn't hit?
I guess he didn't get to dat last bender wid de wood,
An' wasn't I just tellin' you I knowed de hobo could?
Three runs across de bloomin' plate, and now de scrap's a cinch;
Dere never was a guy like him to clout one in a pinch;
Right on de nose across de lot, beyond de outfield's reach,
An' wasn't I just tellin' you dat lobster was a peach?

II.

Say, maybe dis ain't pie to-day wid Mickey on de hill;
Dey couldn't beat dat sucker if he handed 'em de pill;
He ain't lost one in fourteen weeks, and any time dey get
A base hit when he's workin' right just sue me for de debt.
You've got to hand it to him, Bo, and dat's no foolish tip,
He makes dose bloomin' batters look like chickens wid de pip;
I'll take me bonnet off to him—he's kept us in de race,
Fer minus him I'd bet me coat we'd be in seventh place.

Two doubles and a base on balls here in de openin' round?
I wonder why de manager leaves dat mutt on de mound?
Another hit, another pass! See here, you crazy lout,
Why don't you warm a *pitcher* up and take dat bone-head out?
Who said dat guy could pitch a ball? Dere goes another pass.
Dat mucker ain't got smoke enough to crack a pane of glass.
De minute he walked in de box I knowed we'd hit the ditch
An' wasn't I just tellin' you dat hobo couldn't pitch?

THE LOVE SONNETS OF A SON OF SWAT.

I.

TAKE it from me, this Single League's shine,
   My heart got batted from the box to-day;
   For when we met, the dope says right away:
"She bats .300 on the Peaches' Nine."
I'd draft her now, if I thought she would sign
   And help me divvy up a season's pay.
   I pitched this at her, but my grandstand play
Went wild. Says she: "No bush league dub for mine."

Say, she's the big league kid, or I'm a skate;
   For every time I com up—zip, like that,
She shoots those lamps of hers across the plate,
   And I strike out, like Casey on a bat;
For when she curves one over from those eyes,
"Three strikes and out" is just about my size.

II.

Speaking of curves, say, on the level, Bo,
   She'd make Waddell look like a dinky-dink.
   And Eddie Reulbach's straight without a kink;
For she's all curves from neck four feet below—
Out-curves and in-shoots, all there in a row.
   Compared to hers, Ed Plank's are on the blink.
   If Hughey Jennings sees her, I don't think
"Wild Bill" next year will get a chance to show.
I've played some games that I tried hard to win;

But this is my world's series championship;
And if I lost, back to the minor bin
For your young uncle—that's my one best tip.
To-night I'll call, and risk an awful freeze
By showing her just how to work the "squeeze."

III.

Say, I'm the lemon league on a slump;
In love's ball game the bench is where I sit.
I couldn't foul one, must less make a hit
Or tie the game up with a timely thump.
I had a chance to make good on the jump;
But when I tried to grab her little mitt,
I dropped it first, and then I fumbled it,
Playing the game like some bone-headed chump.

But when at last I got my eye and tried
To work the "squeeze," she coached me to my place.
"Get back," she warbled. "Slide, you lobster, slide;
Don't take too long a lead from off your base:
Just play it safe, you mutt; first time at bat
Is not the place to spring a play like that."

IV.

This game of love is not my longest suit;
Doping it out has put wheels in my bun.
Just as you think you've got the pennant won,
Bum luck will land you on the soapy chute;
You come back hard, but every time you boot
Each chance you get until the game is done;

And when at last you need the tying run,
There ain't no bleacher bugs to rise and root.
I doped it out the first time that we faced
To warm up good until I got control,
And then to curve a fast one round her waist,
Hoping this way to put her in a hole.
Such was my dope; but, as I've said before,
The dope is not what makes the full box score.

V.

Ah, love, indeed thou art a heartless game.
The gong rings out, the umpire shouts, "Play ball!"
You rush out gaily till you hear her call:
"Back up, back up, your salary whip is lame.
What batting average stands against your name
In Dun's or Bradstreet's little 'Guide to All?'
You can't tag love inside a cottage wall
Minus the gate receipts—not with this dame!"

"Nix, not for mine," says she. "Fine chance to win
We'd have with landlord on the rival team,
With grocer, butcher fielding up our tin
And smashing liners into love's young dream.
Yours for a steady job and no fatigue
Before I sign with any Fireside League."

VI.

Much like the mutt with home plate well in sight,
Who sprints on in with long, stake-winning stride,
Bringing the tying run with bulging pride;

As hope once more soars upward, like a kite
Who thinks he's got it beat all right, all right;
   While thousands clamor: "Hit the dirt, there—slide!"
   When over all the tumult, far and wide,
The umpire shrieks, "You're out!" in mad delight.

So I got mine in true O'Loughlin style:
   Just when I thought the game would be a tie
Her old man yelled, "You're out about a mile,"
   And waved me back with murder in his eyes.
"I'm acting umpire in this park," says he;
"So don't you pass no funny talk with me."

VII.

So moves life's game wherever we may go;
   At every base some umpire stands and waits—
   A delegate shipped earthward by the fates—
Who has it in for players here below.
We drive one safe inside three feet or so;
   The robber umpire struts around and states
   That "it went foul." We know his eyes ain't mates;
But "foul" it stands, and so the score books go.

But I ain't through. Perhaps in nineteen eight,
   If I can act like Tyrus Cobb at bat,
I'll get a chance to sign a running mate
   And pitch my park within a two-room flat.
Five thousand per might clear her old man's vision
And make him change that other bum decision.

AT THE END OF THE GAME.

WHEN I have heard the Final Umpire's call
 Ring out across the diamond of my strife
 That ends the little game which we call life,
I shall not care about the score at all,
How well I fielded, how I hit the ball;
 Nor all the cheering and the tumult rife,
 Nor shouts of scorn that once cut like a knife—
These shall not matter in the endless pall;

These shall not matter on that final day
 When life's game passes with the setting sun,
If I but hear the Mighty Umpire say:
 "The records show no pennant you have won,
No brilliant average that brings you fame;
Yet you go up, because 'you played the game.'"

"Come, enter quick," St. Peter then replied;
"Heaven's joys to such as you are not denied."

THE MOGUL'S DREAM.

(With apologies to "The Actor's Dream.")

ONE night a mogul died, and straight his soul
Set forth upon its journey to the goal
Of all good people. But the gate was locked;
So while he shivered in the cold, he knocked—
Not once, but twice—he rapped with all his might
Upon the pearly entrance, barred and tight.

"Who comes," St. Peter cried, "with all that din?"
"It's me," the magnate cried. "Please let me in."
"And who are you," he heard the good saint say,
"That you should hear the golden harps, I pray?
What have you done upon that earth so drear,
That you should mingle with the angels here?"
"I was the manager," he straight replied—
"The mogul of a ball team ere I died."

"And what means that," replied the saint, "pray tell?"
"It means that all you ever get is—well,
I won't repeat the word I had in mind;
And yet no other fits that I can find.
Through fall and winter every year I plan
To gather in a pennant-winning clan;
I labor hard from early morn till night
In search of talent anywhere in sight;
Right off the reel, my pitchers one by one
Blow up, and then my catchers are undone;
And for my trouble, what get I in thanks?
The fiendish yelp of twenty thousand cranks.

My life was one of fiendish, piercing woe,
The roughest on that unkempt plain below;
Aye, to the full I've drunk life's bitter dregs—
Hissed, jeered at, pelted with decrepit eggs.
And to what end I come back in the spring?
Only to hear the anvil chorus ring.

L'Envoi.

"Come, enter quick," St. Peter then replied;
"Heaven's joys to such as you are not denied;
Choose any harp among these scenes of mirth.
O HAPLESS SOUL, YOU HAD YOUR HELL
ON EARTH!

HARD-LUCK ADAM.

ADAM had no Easter hat to buy for Mrs. Eve;
Adam had no "cost-of-living" troubles to aggrieve;
Adam had no job to hold by slaving day or night,
Adding columns, beating carpets, planning stuff to
  write.
Adam had a hectic cinch, played across the boards—
Everything that nature and an idle life affords.
And yet I wouldn't change with him, whatever be my
  loss;
He never saw a triple drive the winning run across.

Adam had no dress to buy to calm his spouse's grief
(All that Adam had to do was go and pull a leaf).
Back in Father Adam's day, long and long ago,
There was not an Aldrich nor a crusty Uncle Joe;
Raving politicians never roamed about the land,
Double-crossing voters in a way to beat the band,
But with it all poor Adam never had a chance to dream
Of bold three-hundred hitters and a pennant-winning
  team.

Adam lived on Easy Street, dreaming in the sun;
Never a policeman there to cut in on his fun;
Never had a cook around threatening to leave;
"Bridge" was not invented in the days of Mrs. Eve.
Take it up and down the line in those golden days,
Adam had it on us in a hundred different ways;
And yet with all his blessings, what a dull and massive
  pall—
For poor old Father Adam never saw a game of ball!

DENTON (CY) YOUNG.

(The Grand Old Man of Balldom faces his twentieth season as a major league slabman with every indication that it will be among his best campaigns.)

FAME may be fleeting and glory may fade;
  Life at its best is a breath on the gale.
One hero passes, another is made;
  New stars arise as the old one sets pale.
So when a stalwart steps out from the throng,
  On with the tribute, let garlands be flung.
Here's to the sturdy and here's to the strong;
  Here's to the king of them all, Denton Young.

Anson has passed like a star in the night;
  Richardson's name from the line-up is cast;
Rusie and Latham are out of the fight;
  Mighty Buck Ewing is buried and passed;
Clarkson the wizard, and Kelly and Gore
  Linger no more on the fan's fickle tongue.
Only one name flashes out as of yore—
  There on the red line of battle is Young.

Tiernan and Tucker? We wait for reply.
  Jack Ward and Pfeffer are out of the game;
No cheer arises when Brouthers steps by;
  Even Van Haltren is only a name;
Meekin and Hoffer and "Kind Bid" McPhee—
  Their day is over, their songs are all sung.
Lo! like the roar of the storm-harried sea
  Swells the wild chorus for Denton (Cy) Young.

Denton (Cy) Young.

Herman Long's only a memory now;
   Big Del is under the myrtle to-day—
No more the laurel is bound to his brow;
   Bob Lowe and Zimmer have passed from the fray.
Where are the heroes saluted of old—
   Heroes to whom through the years we have clung?
Have all deserted the Clan of the Bold?
   Not while the echoes are ringing for Young.

Breitenstein, Phillips, and Weyhing and Nops,
   Hahn, Rhines, and Corbett and Dr. McJames—
Where are their shoots and their puzzling drops?
   Who cheers to-day when you mention their names?
Lost in the shadows, their story is told;
   On memory's ramparts their pictures are hung;
But here in the lime light, as great as of old,
   Looms up the stalwart—the only Cy Young.

Where is the mighty Dalrymple to-day?
   Miller and Denny and "Cuppy the Sly?"
Show me their names in the line-up, I pray
   Vainly I wait for an answering cry.
Few of us stand to the guns through the years;
   One at a time from the heights we are flung.
Heroes soon pass in this Valley of Tears;
   But here's to the king of them all—Denton Young.

THE UMP'S MIDWINTER DREAM.

It was a sunny day in spring;
The warbling birds were all a-wing;
An April sky of azure hue
Enchanted the fanatic's view,
And sultry was the atmosphere
Upon the first game of the year.
Upon the field His Umps appeared,
And, lo! the throng arose and cheered,
While all around the fife and drums
Played "Hail! the Conquering Hero Comes."

The game began, and to the plate
The first man wandered up, sedate;
"Strike one, strike two, strike three—you're out!"
The umpire waited for the shout
Of rage from all around, but not
A murmur bubbled from the lot;
The player bowed and walked away,
Without another word to say;
Nor paused, with language somewhat free
Impugning his ancestral tree.
Nobody had a kick to make,
However costly his mistake;
And when a foul tip off the bat
Came hurling by and knocked him flat,
In sympathy the bleachers sat
With saddened hearts and tear-dimmed eyes,
Until once more they saw him rise.
He was to player and to fan

A scholar and a gentleman,
While every paper in the land
Was boosting him to "beat the band."

And then in joy he gave a shout,
And woke to FIND HIS PIPE WAS OUT!

A REAL JOB FOR TEDDY.

TEDDY, when your work is through in the Presidential chair;
When another takes the shift where you've learned to do and dare,
You will need another job—one that's a monstrosity,
That will soak up, day by day, all your strenuosity.
It must be a husky job, full of smoke and fire to boot;
And in looking round I've found only one I know will suit,
Only one where your big stick will be needed day by day;
Only one to fit in, Ted, with your rough-and-tumble way;
Only one where in the end you will some day long for rest,
Where your energy will wane and your spirit be depressed.

You will find it different from any "nature-faking" fuss;
You will find it harder than mauling up the Octopus.
It will be a rougher job than a charge up San Juan Hill,
Or a battle with the trusts—it will take a stronger will.
Fighting predatory wealth of the kings of high finance,
Calling railroad moguls down will not be a circumstance.

All in all, 'twill suit you fine. Never having been
afraid
Of aught else upon this earth, you should be an
umpire, Ted!

That's the only job for you; take our tip now,
Theodore;
Think of how your pulse will leap when you hear the
angry roar.
There your nerve can have full play; you will find the
action there
Which you've hunted for in vain from your Presiden-
tial chair.

Chasing Afric lions and such, catching grizzlies will
seem tame
Lined up with the jolt you'll get in the thick of some
hard game.
Choking hungry wolves to death as a sport will stack
up raw
When you see Kid Elberfield swinging for your
under jaw.
When you hear Hugh Jennings roar, "Call them
strikes, you lump of cheese!"
Or McGraw comes rushing out, kicking at your shins
and knees;
When the bleachers stand and shout, "Robber, liar,
thief, and dub!"
You'll be sorry for the gents in your Ananias Club.
You'll find it's a different thing from making peace
with old Japan

Than when you've called a strike on O'Conner or
McGann.
Holding California back isn't quite the same, I'll
state,
As is calling Devlin out on a close one at the plate.
Though I've hunted far and near, there is nothing
else to do
Where you'll get what's coming, Ted, all that's com-
ing unto you.
You should be an umpire, Ted; and I'll bet two weeks
would be
Quite enough to curb your rash, headlong stren-u-
os-i-tee.

THE SHOCK.

(From "The Revery of an Umpire," with apologies to Ben King's "Ghost.")

IF I should die to-night,
 And as with folded arms in death I lay,
Arrayed in shrouds of linen pure and white,
 Some rooter should bend over me and say,
"Old boy, I'm sorry that you're down and out;
I hope you'll get to heaven, for you're square;
I've seen you umpire many a hard-fought bout
Without one bum decision, I can swear—"

If he said that,
Although my soul was even then a spook,
I'd rise at once in my large, white cravat,
To get one look at him, one final look;
I'd make him pass me out that dope once more,
 The same quaint words that he had used before.
Yes, I'd rise up till he was done, and then—
 I'd drop back dead again.

WHEN "WIFEY" READS DOPE.

SEATED at the breakfast table on a sultry summer's day,
Mrs. Smith picked up the paper in a careless, idle way,
Threw her lamps on social items, noted quickly up and down
Names of lucky, favored people who had blown away from town
In this steamy August weather, till at last her restless glance
Fell upon the sporting section, and she lingered in a trance.

Mr. Smith was eating bacon—which the same, as you should know,
Is a widespread breakfast fodder anywhere you choose to go—
And his jaw was working deftly, like the handle of a pump,
When he heard an exclamation from his wife that made him jump.
"What's the matter?" he responded, with his appetite well sated.
"Why those frowns upon your forehead? Why those eyeballs so dilated?"

"Tell me this," she said and shuddered, "tell me what this means, I pray:
'Nothing but the gallant playing of Mike Johnson saved the day.

With the score tied in the seventh, and the combat
gliding by,
Mike dashed out, and by fast sprinting swallowed Piggy
Jones' long fly.'"
"Good for Mike," her husband answered. "He's the
goods—I always knew it."
"Swallowed Jones's fly?" she murmured. "Tell me how
the man could do it!"

Then she read: "With mighty bludgeons in their mitts,
the demon Sox
Hopped on Waddell in the pinches, hammered him out
of the box,
Shot him full of poisoned arrows, drove him to the
uncut woods,
Walloped all the wadding from him—for he didn't have
the goods."
"This is awful," said she, frowning. "Why should he
have drawn a beating?"
But her husband only snickered, and again turned to his
eating.

"Look at this," she stammered, paling: "'Hahn got
bumped upon the bean;
Umpire Sheridan's decisions threw a smell like gasoline;
Jones was punctured in the lattice; Walsh's benders
broke their backs—
For they couldn't even hit him with a shotgun or an ax.'
Baseball must be very wicked," said she with puzzled face.
"Yes, it's hell," her husband answered, "when your team
ain't in the race."

A HARD-LUCK YARN.

WHILE reposin' one day in me leisurely way, a-puffin' a wicked cheroot,
I happens to spy with a glance of me eye a gent in a major league suit.
"I know who ye are—you're a major league star," says I, "or you once used to be."
"Well, jigger me neck, but your dope is correck," was the answer he handed to me.

And he mutters, says he: "I've a story for ye
Which I want ye to put in the paper for me.

'Twas quite a while back, if me dope is exack, when I was a bloomin' recruit;
I had just busted in from a minor league bin, with a try at a major league suit,
When the followin' tale, which will make you turn pale, happened one day to me in a game;
And I think you'll agree when you hear it from me, that I wasn't hardly to blame.

'Twas the opening fray of the season that day, and the bases was full as a goat;
And the pitcher he smiled in a manner which riled as I swallowed a lump in me throat;
And he winged one across with a deft, easy toss, and it bubbled along at me waist;
And I swung till me back give a horrible crack, but I give it a terrible paist.

That ball riz and sailed till the people all paled, when it
turned to a vanishin' speck;
And me hands was swelled up like a fat, poisoned pup,
while the bat I used was a wreck.
Clean over the ocean, like lightnin' in motion, it whiz-
zled and whistled and whirled;
Over China, Japan, it bounded and ran, till it traveled
the length of the world.

With a most vicious swipe it dismantled the pipe in the
mouth of King Edward at tea;
Then it veered to the Rhine, where it busted a stein
which der Kaiser was holdin', you see;
And it give quite a jar to the badly scared Czar when it
toppled his throne to the ground;
But it went on its way with the speed of H. Bay, with a
hop and a skip and a bound.

That night, with a sigh and a tear in his eye, the cap-
tain give me my release;
For the President wired that I had to be fired for the
good of the country and peace.
'He hits 'em too hard and too fur from the yard,' was
the message the President sent.
'He has raised complications with neighborly nations;
and I am a peaceable gent.'

So they turned me adrift and I give up my shift; and
that's why I'm out of the game.
I was too bloomin' good, or I'm certain I would have
acquired quite a notable name."

A FAN'S DIARY.

(March Fifteenth.)

WE have the greatest team this year beneath the shining sun.
I've studied up the dope on them, yes, every blooming one.
Our fielders are spectacular; and you will throw a fit
When you discover how this bunch can play the game and hit.

Our manager, Mike Johnson, is the only one best bet;
He knows exactly what to do, and what new men to get.
They say he is a wonder at developing a team;
And on the side he always has some pennant-winning scheme.

Jack Smith's a star at second base, while Jones is great at third;
Young Riley is a Matthewson, and Jackson is a bird;
You'll never find a better pair upon the firing line—
The very ones to give this town a pennant-winning nine.

There's no more use in talking, we have got the old flag cinched;
I can see that banner waving, with the pennant good as pinched.
Right from the start it looks to me a runaway this year;
I hope we don't break up the race (this is my only fear).

A Fan's Diary.

(April Fifteenth.)

Hurrah! The season's started—the opening game's to-
day!
The fans are swarming to the park to see our heroes
play;
The whole darn town is turning out, to get in on the
fun
And cheer the team that has the flag already good as
won.

They have a silver loving cup for Johnson, and a cane
For every other player—O, they're raving, wild, insane!
They're cheering like Comanches, all impatient for the
fray,
To see our team jump in and take the lead on opening
day.

(May Fifteenth).

Cheer up, the race ain't over yet, although our
prospect's frayed.
What matter if the team has dropped the first twelve
games they've played?
It makes no difference, rooters, that we're on the bot-
tom rung;
Remember, fans, before you knock, the season's very
young.

(June Fifteenth.)

Say, Johnson, fire that Riley; he's a lemon through and
through.

Who told you Smith could play the game? And Jones is rotten too.
Can that big dub Jackson NOW, and throw him off the nine;
The infield you have signed for us is something of a shine.

(July First.)

I've seen some awful yellow teams in my day, I'll admit;
But say, this bunch can't catch a cold; they neither field nor hit.
Say, this is on the level: I could not believe my eyes
The day I saw that outfield squad drop fourteen easy flies.

When a shortstop makes twelve errors in one game, he's getting stale;
The time has come to ride him out of town upon a rail;
And when a pitcher passes up a dozen men per game,
I wouldn't like to say it, but I KNOW his proper name.

(July Fifteenth.)

Say, fire that Johnson right away, you guys that own the club;
He's nothing but a wooden-headed, drunken, brain-less dub.
He's a holy show as manager, as I said from the first;
You've got to hand it to him as the one and only worst.

A Fan's Diary.

(October First.)

Hurrah! the season's over, and I'm glad the race is past.
I know we finished in the rut this year, a hopeless last.
We didn't do a blooming thing but hit the chutes and
slump;
But NEXT year keep your eye on us—we'll be there
from the jump.

GAME CALLED.

"GAME called"—across the field of play
The dusk has come, the hour is late;
The fight is done and, lost or won,
The player files out through the gate;
The tumult dies, the cheer is hushed,
The stands are bare, the park is still;
But through the night there shines the light
Of Home beyond the silent hill.

"Game called"—where in the golden light
The bugle rolled the reveille,
The shadows creep where night falls deep
And taps has called the end of play;
The game is done, the score is in,
The final cheer and jeer have passed,
But in the night beyond the fight
The player finds his rest at last.

"Game called"—upon the field of life
The darkness gathers, far and wide;
The dream is done, the score is spun
That stands forever in the guide;
Nor victory, nor yet defeat
Is chalked against the player's name,
But down the roll the final scroll
Shows only "how he played the game."

Index of Titles and First Lines

Index of Titles and First Lines